The Resurrection Mouse

Phyllis Didleau
Illustrated by Gretchen Gackstatter

© 2014, 2021 by Phyllis Constant Didleau
All Rights Reserved. First edition published 2014.

The Resurrection Mouse
Second edition, August 1, 2021. Previously published by Mother's House Publishing, Inc.
Original illustrations in watercolor by Gretchen Gackstatter

Published by BOOK BOOK SQUARED
P.O. Box 60144
Colorado Springs, Colorado 80960

Printed in the United States of America

ISBN 978-1-943829-38-5

www.goldenrulemasterpieces.com
www.mangermouse.com

BOOK BOOK SQUARED is an imprint of Rhyolite Press, LLC

To My Risen Savior, Jesus Christ

Near a hill outside the city of Jerusalem
a mouse family lived.

They were a busy, happy family
always looking for olives, dates, and figs
for breakfast, lunch, and dinner.

On one warm, bright day as they scurried around the hill they heard a hard, sharp sound.
They were puzzled.

It was like that of a hammer hitting a nail.

Scampering closer to the sound, they saw an angry crowd gathering.

It appeared to them that the crowd was bringing a wounded, beaten man to the hill.

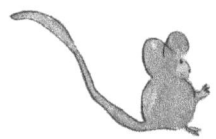

They carefully moved to hide under a large rock so no one in the hateful crowd could see them.

The mouse family saw the man named
Jesus with bruises and cuts all over his
body. Several of the men had placed a crown of
thorns upon his head and now were nailing him
to a large, wooden cross.

That's when the sound came again—this time it was the sound of a man being hurt by the nasty group. The little mouse family began to cry and felt very sad as they saw all this happening.

They dug further and further under the rock
hoping to get into a place where they couldn't see
or hear this sadness anymore.

Hard as they tried to get away, they could still hear the hurting man. They clearly heard him say, "Father, forgive them for they know not what they do."

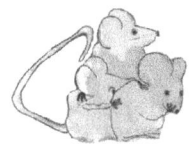

"What kind of man would say something like that after all they did to him?" Father mouse questioned. "He must be a god-like man. Yes, He must be God."

They heard a soldier exclaim,
"Truly, He is the son of God!"

Suddenly darkness came over the whole land and the earth shook and rocks split. "Oh, my goodness," Father mouse trembled with fright. "What, oh, what, has happened?"

They then heard the voice of a woman. "Come, let us follow Joseph to the tomb where Jesus will be buried. Then let us go home and prepare spices and perfumes. After our day of rest, which is Saturday, we will prepare his body for burial."

The little family of mice scampered out from under the huge rock. They saw Joseph, a good man from the little town of Arimathea, take the body of Jesus. He wrapped Jesus in linen cloth and placed Him in the tomb.

Carefully the little mouse family scampered inside the tomb to be near the Son of God. There was a spirit of joy in the tomb and a feeling that all was well. A huge stone was rolled across the opening of the burial place.

As morning came on the third day, the mice saw that the huge stone was gone. Jesus was gone, too. They saw women coming from a distance.

Suddenly the earth moved and small rocks tumbled down the hillside, frightening the little mouse family.

An angel appeared. The angel was bright as lightning. His clothes were glowing. The mice heard him say to the alarmed women, "Do not be afraid, for I know you are looking for Jesus who was nailed to the cross. He is not here.
He is risen! Just as He said.
He has risen from the dead!"

Father mouse turned to his wife mouse and children with an amazed and joyful look on his face. Father mouse shouted, "He was dead and now He is alive! No one on earth can come alive once they have died! This man called Jesus is alive! Oh, I am so excited! We must tell everyone of this event. We must tell everyone. Jesus, who is most certainly God, is alive!"

From that day forward, everyone the mouse family visited was told the story that Jesus is risen, Jesus is alive, Jesus is resurrected!

This cross you see here is to remind you that you, too, must tell the story! You must tell the story because you know the story! You must tell the story that the little Resurrection Mouse told! You must tell everyone that Jesus is alive! You must!

The author, Phyllis Constant Didleau, holds a Bachelor Degree with a Life Certificate in elementary education from the University of Northern Colorado in Greeley. As a postgraduate student, she studied in Special Education at the University of Hawaii in Honolulu. Phyllis has many years experience in the classroom.

As a high school student she taught Sunday School and has been the Director of Children's Church. She has provided years of volunteering teaching children and participating in Vacation Bible School. Her Biblical studies include a two-year course from the Institute of Theology by Extension through the Department of International Studies, Open Bible Churches.

Gretchen Gackstatter, the illustrator, received a Bachelor Degree in Fine Arts from the University of Northern Colorado, Greeley. Over the years, she has taught art from kindergarten through high school. At the present time she teaches watercolor at the Argonne Gallery in St. Louis, Missouri. Her watercolors have gained a wide, popular reputation.

www.ingramcontent.com/pod-product-compliance
Lightning Source LLC
LaVergne TN
LVHW072126090426
835512LV00039B/3487